W9-AST-022

HAITI

An Imprint of Scholastic Library Publishing
Danbury, Connecticut

Published for Grolier
an imprint of Scholastic Library Publishing
Old Sherman Turnpike, Danbury, Connecticut 06816
by Marshall Cavendish Editions
an imprint of Marshall Cavendish International
1 New Industrial Road, Singapore 536196

Set ISBN: 0-7172-5788-6
Volume ISBN: 0-7172-5792-4

Library of Congress Cataloging-in-Publication Data
Haiti.
p. cm.—(Fiesta!)
Summary: Discusses the festivals and holidays of Haiti and how the songs, food,
and traditions associated with these celebrations reflect the culture of the people.
1. Festivals—Haiti—Juvenile literature. 2. Haiti—Social life and customs—Juvenile literature.
[1. Festivals—Haiti. 2. Holidays—Haiti. 3. Haiti—Social life and customs.]
I. Grolier (Firm). II. Fiesta! (Danbury, Conn.)
GT4826.A2H35   2004
394.267294—dc21   2003044842

For this volume
Author: Maude Heurtelou
Editor: Paul A. Rozario
Designer: Geoslyn Lim
Production: Nor Sidah Haron
Crafts and Recipes produced by Stephen Russell

Printed by Everbest Printing Co. Ltd

Adult supervision advised for all crafts and recipes,
particularly those involving sharp instruments and heat.

CONTENTS

HAITI:

Haiti is located on the mountainous island of Hispaniola in the Caribbean Sea. The original people of Haiti were indigenous Indians called Tainos. The name "Haiti" comes from the Taino word "Ayiti," which means "land of many mountains."

ATLANTIC OCEAN

Môle Saint Nicolas

Île de la Gonâve

Jérémie

Jamaica Channel

Miragoâne

Les Cayes

CARIBBEAN SEA

▲ **The Citadelle La Ferrière** is a fortress that was built in the early 1800s in northern Haiti. Workers carried stones, rocks, gravel, and bronze cannons to the top of the mountain on which it was built.

▶ **Cap-Haïtien** is the second largest city in the country. During the 1600s Cap-Haïtien was the wealthiest of all the colonial cities of France. Today it is a beautiful port city on Haiti's northern coast.

4

Tortuga Island

Port-de-Paix

Cap-Haïtien

Grande Riviére du Nord

Gonaïves

Saint Marc

Artibonite

DOMINICAN REPUBLIC

Etang Saumâtre

Port-au-Prince Bay

Pétionville

PORT-AU-PRINCE

La Selle (8,793 ft)

Jacmel

▲ **The Royal Palm** is a large tropical tree with a tall trunk and large leaves. The tree symbolizes victory and success for the Haitian people, and it can be found on Haiti's flag.

▶ **The Unknown Maroon** is a statue built near the president's palace in Port-au-Prince, the capital of Haiti. It was built in memory of the Haitian slaves who rebelled in 1791. To prepare for the revolt, the rebels communicated their plans to each other by blowing on a conch shell, sending special code sounds.

RELIGIONS

The majority of Haitians are Roman Catholics, while the remainder belong to Protestant churches. A small number of Haitians follow other religions or have none at all. Most Haitians, including Catholics and Protestants, also practice at least some customs of a religion called voodoo.

MOST HAITIANS celebrate Christian festivals such as Christmas, Easter, All Souls' Day, and All Saints' Day. They also celebrate events such as baptisms and first communions. These events often end with a reception and a dancing party.

Voodoo has its roots in African beliefs. When Africans of various tribes were brought to Haiti as slaves, they brought with them beliefs in different spirits. In time, the various different African beliefs and rituals combined to form the voodoo religion. Believers claim to be able to talk with spirits called *lwa* or *loa*. The ceremonies or rituals are led by a voodoo priest. Services include long songs and dances. Voodoo rituals show some Catholic influences such as blessings, the sign of cross, and kneeling

During voodoo ceremonies artistic patterns called vévé are drawn on the floor with cornmeal. These vévé patterns are also embroidered on cloth.

down. Voodoo has also had bad publicity. Scary books and movies have used the word voodoo to refer to rituals and beliefs that are not part of the religion. Voodoo is a religion just like any other religion and should be respected just like any other religion.

Most Haitians are Catholics and celebrate Christmas. These Haitian angles are used to decorate Christmas trees.

GREETINGS FROM **HAITI!**

The two official languages of Haiti are French and Haitian Creole. All Haitians speak Haitian Creole, but only 10 percent of the population speaks French as well. French is the language of the government. Some linguists believe that Haitian Creole originated when French slave masters needed a way to talk to the slaves and the slaves with each other. Even though Haitian Creole was most likely based on French, it is very different from French and has more similarities to West African languages.

How do you say...

How are you?
Kouman ou ye?

Good morning, ladies and gentlemen
Bonjou, mesyedam

Have a nice day
Pase bòn jounen

See you later
Orevwa

7

NEW YEAR'S DAY

New year's Day is celebrated all over the world, but in Haiti it is also the country's Independence Day. In Port-au-Prince the day starts with a religious service at the cathedral. It is followed by a 21-cannon salute that is heard throughout the city. The celebrations then begin in all the towns and villages in Haiti.

In every household the aroma of steaming pumpkin soup rises from the kitchen early in the morning. Every Haitian eats pumpkin soup on New Year's Day. Some say it's because pumpkin soup was a forbidden dish for their ancestors when they were enslaved. This tradition is even practiced by Haitians living outside Haiti.

New Year's Day is one of the greatest days of the year for Haitian children. After eating their soup, they change into new outfits and shoes. Then they visit their neighbors to wish them a happy New Year. The neighbors are happy to serve the children cakes and homemade drinks. The neighbors also give the children money or other gifts.

New Year's Day is also the day on which people who have had an argument forgive each other, shake hands, and start their friendship all over. It's also the day many people voice their wishes for the year.

Pumpkin soup is a traditional dish in Haiti during New Year celebrations.

8

Later in the afternoon most people go to the main park of their town to listen to the band play music and to watch the *masuife*. The *masuife* is a popular New Year's Day tradition. The aim is to climb to the top of a waxed pole to get the money that has been put there.

Many people climb only halfway up the pole before sliding down. It can take the whole night before one of the men is successful.

Colorful flowers are often used to decorate homes during Haitian festivals.

PUMPKIN SOUP

SERVES EIGHT

12 oz of beef meat containing bone
3 lbs of pumpkin, peeled, seeded, and cut in large cubes
2 big carrots, peeled and finely chopped
1 medium turnip, peeled and cubed
1 stalk of celery, coarsely chopped
2 small taro
2 medium potatoes, peeled and cubed
4 sorrel leaves, finely chopped
A sprig of parsley
1 tbsp of salt
3 cloves
1 tsp of thyme
1 lime, juiced
4 garlic cloves, finely chopped
1 large onion, coarsely chopped
1 tbsp of olive oil
1 tbsp of butter
1/4 tsp of ground pepper
1 jalapeno pepper (optional)
6 cups of water

1 Put the water in a pot, and add the meat with the salt, cloves, thyme, lime juice, ground pepper, and garlic.

2 Let it boil on medium heat for half hour or until the meat is tender.

3 Add the squash, carrots, onion, turnip, celery, taro, potatoes, sorrel leaves, salt, and 4 more cups of hot water.

4 Cover, and let steam.

5 Stir the soup every 10 minutes after it starts boiling to keep it from sticking to the bottom of the pot.

6 When the squash is tender, remove it, and mash it well.

7 Add two cups of boiling water to the mashed squash, stir, and pour it back into the soup.

8 Cover on medium heat for 30 minutes.

9 When the stock has reduced in volume, add the parsley.

10 Put in the olive oil, the butter, and the jalapeno pepper.

11 Add salt to taste. Reduce heat to low, stir every 10 minutes for 30 minutes or until satisfied with the thickness of the soup.

CARNIVAL!

Carnival is a fun time in Haiti. It is celebrated during three days in February or March. The end of Carnival marks the beginning of Lent.

Rehearsals for Carnival usually start in January and last for several weeks until February or March. During rehearsals, if you hear a frequent whistle blowing early in the morning, you know that there may be a *madigra*, a *lamayót*, or a *chaloska* coming close to your house to entertain people. The *madigra* are just real people dressed up in the funniest way, with their faces covered with

During Carnival many people wear colorful masks. These masks can be of different animals or of frightening creatures that look like monsters from the imagination.

masks. They stroll in the streets, blowing their whistles to let children know they are passing by.

It's hard to say whether the *lamayót* are funny or scary. It depends on what they carry in the box under their arm. Brave children sometimes call them for a show. Once a *lamayót*

responds to a call and gets ready for a show, children from the immediate neighborhood come to see what surprise there is in his box. The *lamayót* gets the audience excited by what he says, sings, or does. By the end of the show he opens his box, and the whole crowd of children

People who walk in the Carnival procession have to wear bright clothes with many feathers and beads. These costumes can take many months to make.

and adults scream at the top of their lungs. The surprise can be a little mouse happy to get out of the box or nothing at all. Then the *lamayót* sings a

song and leaves for another part of town.

The *chaloska* are scary. They are real people who wear creepy costumes that frighten children and make them cry. *Chaloska* usually wear scary masks, with long, crooked teeth attached to oversized red gums. In their hands are long, thick cords that they twirl, smacking the paved street with circular motions, and making a loud noise. Some parents don't let their children attend a *chaloska's* show, fearing that they can be hit with the cords, but the *chaloska* are so skilled that they never hit children.

By lunchtime drumbeats can be heard, signaling the arrival of the musical groups and bands. The musicians stand on top of huge floats that move around slowly. The fans gather around the float and walk with it. Every year each musical group and their fans come up with their own themes and usually wear the same colors and symbols. When a band meets another band, they play the *ochan*, a song of friendship during which the floats stop, and the fans take off their colorful hats and swing them in all directions.

11

After such mutual courtesy the two groups separate and continue on their way.

The rehearsal time lasts about six Sundays, and then the real thing starts from *Sunday Gras* to Tuesday, or *Mardi Gras*! You know it is the real thing because people start walking around in their costumes early in the morning. The *madigra*, *lamayót*, and *chaloska* are funnier and scarier on those three days. The

Carnival masks can be made from papier-mâché. Just make sure you make holes in the masks for your nose so that you can breathe easily!

streets are colorfully decorated, waiting for the floats and musical groups with their fans.

By about one o'clock in the afternoon, the musical groups have assembled at the city hall. Each group has its flag. You can tell to which group people belong by what they wear. At two o'clock people who are going to march with their group should already be meeting their team. The procession finally begins at three o'clock. Some people enjoy watching the procession of floats and musical groups from their home balconies. Some line the streets to watch the procession.

Carnival takes place in February or March, when the weather is warm. Straw hats and light clothing protect people who line the streets to watch the procession.

Others watch the festival on television.

The Carnival procession is a three-hour long parade of dance, music, costumes, and beautifully decorated floats. The floats, all elegantly dressed up in multicolored satin fabrics, are transformed into different shapes. On top of the floats beautiful and elegant beauty queens blow kisses and throw free gifts to the crowd.

By the end of the night the floats are parked at city hall, and the musicians go to clubs where adults will continue dancing late into the night. Children go to bed exceptionally late and put aside their costumes so that they can use them on the second and third day of Carnival. Children love Carnival because they can stay up late, go to children's parties, wear funny costumes, and eat lots of food!

Children get to eat lots of sweets and candies during Carnival.

BEIGNETS
MAKES 14 TO 16

1 cup of flour
¾ cup of syrup
2 ripe bananas
1 egg (yolk only)
¼ tsp of cinnamon powder
¼ tsp of nutmeg
¼ tsp of vanilla
¼ tsp of salt
1 cup of milk
2 tsp of baking powder
1 cup of frying oil

Beignet is a favorite Carnival food. It is made from bananas, or plaintains, which are fruits that look like bananas.

1 Mash the bananas.
2 Mix the flour with milk, syrup, mashed bananas, egg yolk, and all the spices.
3 Add the baking powder. Mix well.
4 Pour the oil into a large pan, and wait until it is hot.
5 Add large spoonfuls of the mix one at a time. Let them brown on one side, turn to brown the other side, then put them on a plate, and sprinkle with white sugar. Serve while warm.

MAKE A PAPIER-MÂCHÉ CARNIVAL MASK

YOU WILL NEED

A balloon
Strips of newspaper
Container with clean water
Paint brushes
Glue (art paste or cooked starch or wall paper glue)
A pair of scissors

Masks in Haiti are part of the country's African traditions. Today they are used for fun during Carnival. In ancient times, however, people believed that masks allowed a person to stop being himself or herself and become the spirit of the image represented by the mask.

Masks are often painted and decorated with beads, plant fibers, seeds, shells, and small animal bones. Some are crudely made to be used just for a single occasion. Others are made with leather or wood and are longer-lasting.

Some masks are made with colored paper glued onto a heavy quality paper, which is used to make the desired shape. Some people use *papier-mâché*. Masks can be worn to cover the face only, or some can cover the whole head.

1 Inflate the balloon to about 14 inches in diameter. Mark out the areas for eyes and mouth.

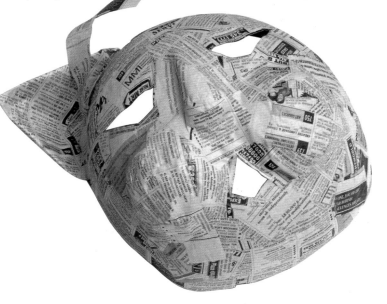

2 Dip individual strips of precut newspaper into the glue mixture. Apply the strips in layers onto about half of the balloon. Smooth the strips as you layer the balloon. Do not cover the eyes and mouth. Leave an area about 5 inches around where the balloon is tied.

3 Repeat the process, adding about four more layers. Let the mask dry.

4 Pop the balloon, and remove it.

5 Make triangle shapes out of the remaining paper strips, and attach to the top of the mask as ears.

6 Paint the type of face you prefer. Use bright and bold colors.

7 Cut or widen the eye and mouth openings.

RARA

Rara bands are groups of musicians, dancers, and ordinary people who take to the streets during Holy Week before Easter and during All Saints' Week in November.

A rara band is different from a carnival band, since you cannot become a member unless you live in the same neighborhood as the band. A rara band is like a club or a kind of association that relies on men and women willing to demonstrate the strength and wealth of their rara band, as well as the beauty and originality of their colorful costumes.

Besides the noisy drums, musicians in rara bands play handmade instruments like the bamboo, the graters, the horns, and long metal cylinders that look like trombones. Their music is based on only four notes, but they are able to produce many different sounds using their handmade instruments.

As rara bands travel on foot through the streets, members swing heavy batons and wave their identifying flags. They also sing specially composed rara songs. They dance with ceremonial gestures and perform complicated patterns as they double back on themselves. Some members smack their batons together. Meanwhile, their leader whips the paved street with heavy cords and whistles in harmony with the creative musicians.

Musicians in rara bands make some of their own instruments, including metal graters, trumpets and wooden maracas.

People on the street are attracted by the haunting bass notes, the scratching percussion sounds of the graters, and the distinctive songs of the singers. They stop to listen and enjoy the exciting atmosphere of a rara band.

When different rara bands meet in the streets, they are cordial with each other. Their respective leaders come forward and salute each other in a friendly way. In the Artibonite area in the center of Haiti the rara bands are so large that they include groups of children, women, adult men, and teenage boys. In Jacmel most bands mix children and adults, men and women.

Spectators and rara fans sometimes will travel miles and miles of dusty roads to visit a town, a region, or a province in Haiti where rara bands are famous. However, so many scary stories have been told about rara bands that most children cover their head with their pillow when they hear a band coming. Just to know that some rara members twirl machetes and carry bones under their arms makes them scarier than Halloween!

Drums are one of the more important instruments in a rara band. They help keep the rhythm going.

17

CAN BOUKI WIN THIS TIME?

Brothers Bouki and Malis are two legendary Haitian characters. They are always getting into some sort of mischief. Many Haitian folktales have the brothers as the main characters, and Haitians love to hear stories about Bouki and Malis during festivals and celebrations.

IT WAS ALL SAINTS' WEEK, and Bouki was getting married. He had met the girl months ago but kept it secret, worried that his brother Malis might win her heart. He informed his mother and Malis about the girl only days before the wedding.

"Why did you choose that day?" his mother asked, "You know that your friends would prefer to go to rara instead!"

Bouki had always been stubborn and shortsighted. His mother couldn't make him change his mind. Bouki insisted that he couldn't change the date. Malis, always cleverer than Bouki, went to meet the girl. It happened that the girl liked Malis better than Bouki and decided to marry Malis instead.

"Don't worry about it," Malis told her. "I will explain everything to Bouki."

Poor Bouki had no idea what was going on. He bought his outfit, got the girl's ring, and scheduled a priest to come celebrate the wedding at the girl's house.

On the wedding day, elegantly dressed Bouki left his house, excited to be doing something that would make Malis envy him for the first time. Then at the first corner he met a rara band. The leader stepped up, shook Bouki's hand, and started cracking his whip around

frightened Bouki, while some members danced all around him. This was quite an honor for Bouki! The band couldn't be ignored, and Bouki danced along.

He was at the next street when another rara band honored him again with the same one-hour ceremony. By the time he got to his bride's house it was one o'clock in the morning, and he had been honored by ten different rara bands. The wedding party was at its end, and the security guard wouldn't let him in. When Bouki insisted that he was the groom, he was arrested and thrown into jail. The girl was already married and on her way to her honeymoon with Malis. Bouki's mother wasn't surprised that Bouki had been fooled again, and she consoled him with the candies and cookies that Malis had sent from the reception. Bouki had no idea that Malis had everything arranged so that all the rara bands in town would delay him while he was on his way to the wedding. He wasn't angry. Instead, Bouki was happy to get something to eat after that long night of dancing!

EASTER SUNDAY FAIR

On Easter Sunday children wear new clothes and put on fancy shoes. Their hair is also styled in a special way. After church many families treat themselves to a rich lunch with turkey. Then they all go to the Easter Sunday Fair.

The fair is at the park nearby where children can go on rides and eat *fresko* and many other goodies. The best of all are the raffles. Raffles are booths where children can try to win a toy, a game, or a surprise gift if they buy a folded ticket. Everyone wants to win,

At the fair children love to drink the soft drinks and eat the sweets, fruits, candies, and ice creams that are on sale.

especially when the prize to be raffled is right there on a table looking at you. Sometimes children buy many tickets with their coins but never get to win.

But it's okay. It is worth a try. After the parents drag their children away from those booths, the children spend some time on the rides and the roller coasters. There is always the temptation to go for ride after ride, but you have to keep going; otherwise, you miss the magician.

The same magician is there every year. He always repeats the same tricks, but none of the children has yet figured out the secret of his magic.

Boys like to attend the *sek* contest. *Sek* is a game of dexterity and balance. It's about keeping a metal circle balanced with a special hanger while rolling the metal circle on the ground and running after it. Somehow, boys seem to do better at it, while the girls beat them in hopscotch.

After doing all that, the children's new outfits are all dirty, and they are tired and sleepy. But they would never agree to go to bed without the traditional ice cream at the parlor. After that they have a nighttime shower and go to bed. This is one night when those who don't snore, snore.

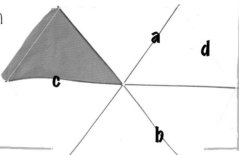

A HAITIAN KITE

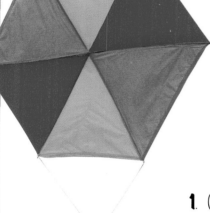

YOU WILL NEED
3 coconut palm stems
Thin thread or string
Thin colorful paper
Paper glue
Light cloth

1. Cut the palm stem pieces to the desired sizes.
2. Note that a, b, and c are of equal size, but "d" is half their size.
3. Assemble the reeds as shown in the drawing.
4. Secure the pieces in position with 3 turns of string at the center, bottom, and side.
5. Secure the end of each reed with string.
6. Cut pieces of fine paper of different colors, and glue them as shown in the drawing.
7. Fold about ⅛ inch of paper over the edges of the kite.
8. Attach a piece of string to hold the cloth tail.
9. Attach the tail to the string.

FLAG DAY

Flag day in Haiti is celebrated on May 18. It's both a major holiday and a special event for students. It is the only holiday when students report to school.

In early May school students begin rehearsals for the Flag Day parade. In class they learn more about Haiti's fight for independence in the late 1800s and their ancestors' struggle for freedom. They also learn about the symbolism of the Haitian flag. The students understand that Haitians are descendants of heroes who fought to end slavery began by the French.

Soon Flag Day is here, and students come to school early in the morning dressed in their sparkling clean school uniforms and shiny black shoes. Some of the girls wear dark blue or red ribbons in their hair. They are the colors of the Haitian flag.

Students and teachers gather in the school courtyard or field. They get ready to march in the direction of the park where the parade will start. In Port-au-Prince, the capital, each school always lines its students up at the Champ de Mars, the park not far from the president's palace. Then they walk to the grounds of the palace with great marching bands ahead of them.

The students who head their school marching groups are honored to carry the large school flag, while the students that follow carry smaller flags. Before and after the parade the president of the country usually delivers a patriotic message. The whole event may take up to four hours under the hot

The Haitian flag shows two bands of blue and red, with a white rectangle in the center that bears the Haitian coat of arms: a palm tree, flags, and two cannons.

summer sun. But no student would ever want to miss it because the Flag Day parade represents the courage and dignity of their Haitian ancestors.

The faces of Haiti's founding fathers, as well as the Haitian coat of arms, can be found on the country's notes and coins.

AYITI CHERI

One of the popular songs played during the flag day parade is Ayiti Cheri.

A- yi- ti   che- ri   pi bon pe- yi pa- se ou nanp-wen   Fúk mwen

te   kite   w pou mwen te kap konprann valé w   Fúk mwen te   man ke w pou

m te   kap apre sye w   Pou m santi   vre-man tout sa ou te ye pou   mwen

SAUT D'EAU

Saut d'Eau is a waterfall located not far from Ville-Bonheur in central Haiti. It is considered a sacred place. Haitians believe that the Virgin Mary appeared there in 1884 in a palm tree. Many people now go to Saut d'Eau on pilgrimage.

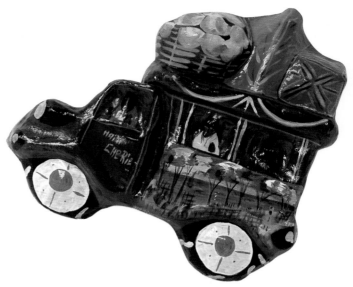

Many Haitians and foreigners from all over the world come to Saut d'Eau to see the 100-foot waterfall, pay homage to the Virgin Mary, or enjoy the festive atmosphere of the town. During the same period Saut d'Eau receives voodoo followers who honor Ersulie Dantor, Goddess Mother of All, during a special ceremony.

The road to Saut d'Eau is bumpy and mountainous. Some people come in cars and trucks. Others come on donkeys or on foot. Children from the cities enjoy the trip to the countryside and the frequents stops along the way to buy food.

There is also great curiosity to see the waterfall and maybe to see the Virgin Mary. Many people go to Saut d'Eau to pray and hope for a miracle for their illnesses. The children go because their parents take them along with them, and they spend the whole time all excited to see the activities around the waterfall.

youngsters make music with a drum, a guitar, and two metal bars that they knock together to keep the beat.

There is a fun atmosphere in Saut d'Eau: no need to be dressed up in shoes too tight or too big; no need to keep your clothes clean, nor will parents scold children for getting dirty; no limit on what you can eat even if you may get sick later. It's so much fun! At night the storyteller arrives and calls everyone under the almond tree. No one wants to miss his stories. And everyone knows that they may not sleep at all until daybreak!

The scene in Saut d'Eau is festive, the crowd huge, and the atmosphere chaotic. Shop stands are set up everywhere. Here, some people sell talismans; there, heavyset ladies make *fritay* (fried plantains) and other popular Haitian dishes. At the waterfall people get into the water for ceremonies and prayers. On the river bank a group of

People all over Haiti travel to Saut d'Eau to see the famous waterfall. Some travel in colorfully painted vans called tap-taps.

SIMBI, QUEEN OF THE WATERS

Haitian legends say that Simbi, Queen of the Waters, lives in an underwater cave somewhere near Saut d'Eau. She is a mystery to the townspeople: Some say she was an Indian queen, others a girl who was forever punished for refusing to love. Some say that she comes up from her cave at night and sits on a rock, where she sings softly and sadly of loneliness while combing her long, beautiful hair.

ONE DAY, NEAR SAUT D'EAU many people were honoring Ersulie Dantor, the Goddess Mother of All. That evening, ten-year-old Amélie was walking very late by the river. Amélie was an orphan. Earlier that day she had been kicked out of her godmother's house because she had lost her godmother's only silver spoon in the river. She begged for forgiveness, but her godmother was so mad at losing her only valuable object that she cursed Amélie and sent her away.

So, while everybody else was celebrating that evening, Amélie was feeling sorry for herself and scared about her future. Walking along the river, she suddenly heard a sweet and lovely singing voice:

Komé Lilin O, lele, lele
Komé Lilin O, lele, lele,
Tiye woch anwo, tiye woch anba,
Lele, lele.

It was Simbi, Queen of the Waters. Amélie was frightened when she saw Simbi; but when the queen called to her "Pssst! Pssst!" she was captivated.

Amélie approached the queen, not even feeling her feet as she moved toward her. Simbi already knew of Amélie's sorrow so she took her to her underwater cave and gave her a whole set of silver spoons and gold nuggets. Amélie was absolutely thrilled and saw an immediate opportunity to take revenge on her godmother.

"Now, my dream of being happy just came true. I am rich. I will buy a castle, I will marry a powerful man, and I will order that he kill my godmother. Thank you, Simbi, for giving me a new life."

But before Simbi brought Amélie back to the world above, she gave Amélie a piece of advice

"You see, Amélie," said the queen, "I learned this the hard way. It is useless to be powerful, rich, and heartless. I killed the only person who ever loved me. Since then I am condemned to never be happy in spite of all my riches. Your godmother was mean for kicking you out, but wasn't she the only person who cared for you when your parents died and you became an orphan? Why don't you go back to her and teach her a lesson about love?"

Simbi then returned Amélie to the world above. Years later Amélie married her true love, and her godmother was right behind her, smiling with joy and pride, and throwing flowers on the path of the happy couple. Even today it is believed that many people come to the waters of Saut d'Eau in search of true love and forgiveness.

COMBITE

A combite takes place in rural Haiti during the planting and harvesting seasons. It's an African tradition. Farmers invite their friends, neighbors, and other farmers to come work for a day, planting seeds or harvesting crops together.

The combite usually starts early in the morning and ends by five in the evening. People who help out are rewarded with food, drinks, and hospitality. When they have finished plowing or harvesting a field, they move on to the next field for the following combite, and that is how work is done every year.

The combite is hard work, and mainly men do the heavy labor. Planting or

This Haitian Tree of Life sculpture, the farmer dolls, and the stone fruit opposite remind us that Haiti is mainly an agricultural country.

harvesting under the sun is difficult and can only be done for a few hours in the morning when the heat of the sun is not too strong. The combite is supervised by a director, and music accompanies the men as they work. Drummers and other musicians play all sorts of music to encourage the workers as they perform the labor.

The workers and farmers use hoes, shovels, rakes, and pickaxes to plow or harvest. Meanwhile, women and children are nearby packing the crops in bags or cooking for the men. Everyone sings in tune with the melodies the musicians play. The atmosphere is very festive. Because everyone cooperates and does their part, the work is soon over in the early evening.

That night a rara is held during which members of a rara band parade, dance, and sing while playing instruments. More dancing and singing continue throughout the night until daybreak.

YELLOW BIRD

The popular song Yellow Bird is based on the tune of Chou Koun, a traditional Haitian folk song that is often sung at Combite.

Yel-low bird, up high in ba-na-na tree.   Did your la-dy friend leave the nest again?   That is ve-ry sad,
Yel-low bird, you sit all a-lone like me.

makes me feel so bad.   You can fly a-way,   in the sky a-way.   You're more luc-ky than   me.

OTHER FESTIVALS

Haiti celebrates many other festivals. These festivals always include singing, dancing, and feasting.

THE ANNIVERSARY OF THE DEATH OF TOUSSAINT L'OUVERTURE is celebrated on April 7. François Dominique Toussaint L'Ouverture was born in Haiti in 1743. Although a slave, Toussaint learned to read because his master was a kind and educated man. After reading stories about military history and battles, Toussaint decided to free his people from slavery. During the slave uprisings of 1791 Toussaint fought the Spanish, the French, the British, and the white landowners of Haiti. He eventually sided with the French, for he felt that would give him the greatest chance to abolish slavery in Haiti. After the war the French made Toussaint governor of Haiti. Once in power, Toussaint outlawed slavery. The French were scared that Haiti would become independent from France. So they captured Toussaint and brought him to France, where he died in prison in 1803.

ALL SOULS' DAY falls on November 2. This day is dedicated to remembering and honoring people who have passed away. On this day Haitians visit the graves of dead relatives and friends. They place flowers on the tombstones and light candles around them, all the while saying prayers and singing songs.

MANGER YAM is a harvest festival celebrated on November 25. During this festival yams are harvested and stored in a sacred place. There they are blessed by a voodoo priest and later distributed to eat. There is much dancing and singing during Manger Yam.

THE DISCOVERY OF HAITI BY CHRISTOPHER COLUMBUS is celebrated on December 5.

Words to Know

Ayiti: Haiti's name prior to its discovery by Columbus.

Beignets: Fried dough made with flour, sugar, ripe bananas, eggs, and spices, and consumed during Carnival.

Chaloska: People dressed in scary costumes carrying cords that they slap on the ground to make loud sounds.

Chaotic: Disorganized, loud, and noisy.

Coat of arms: Figures found on a shield or flag.

Dexterity: To be able to move one's body in an agile way.

Fresko: A dessert with crushed ice and colored syrup.

Fritay: Dish of fried plantains—fruit that looks and tastes like bananas.

Hispaniola: The name of the island shared by Haiti and the Dominican Republic.

Lamayót: An entertainer who tells stories and sing songs. He carries a wooden box with a surprise inside.

Lwa or **loa:** Spirits of the voodoo religion.

Madriga: People wearing clown costumes and masks.

Nuggets: A lump of gold or other precious metal.

Ochan: A musical greeting or exchange between two rara bands.

Papier-mâché: A mixture of glue and strips of newspaper. Papier-mâché hardens as it dries.

Procession: A large group of people moving in an orderly fashion, usually in a line.

Sek: A game in which a circular piece of metal is kept rolling on the ground with a rod.

Supervise: To control or watch over an activity being performed by other poeple.

Vévé: Artistic patterns with vodoo symbolism that are very typical of Haitian art. They are usually reproduced on elaborately embroidered cloth.

ACKNOWLEDGMENTS

WITH THANKS TO:
Maude Heurtelou, Paul Rozario, Emy de Pradines, staff of the Oloffson Hotel, Leah Gordon and the Haiti Support Group (U.K.), Rebecca Hossack and the staff of the London RHG and Windmill Street galleries, and Mr. and Mrs. Richard Morse. All objects in this book belong to the Fondation Sebastien pour l'Art Haïtien, which has kindly allowed reproduction in this instance.

PHOTOGRAPHS BY:
David Simson (cover); Andre Poon; Maude Heurtelou (p. 10 top right, p. 12 top right, p. 25, plant). Eleanor Frank/ Kay Shaw Photography (p. 23, currency).

ILLUSTRATIONS BY:
Lee Kowling (p. 19, p. 27) and Tan Joo Lee (p.1, p. 4-5, p. 7).

SET CONTENTS